AN AFFECTIONATE FAREWELL

The Story of Old Bob and Old Abe

written by Trudy Krisher

illustrated by Bert Dodson

www.bunkerhillpublishing.com
Bunker Hill Publishing, Inc.
285 River Road, Piermont
New Hampshire 03779, USA

10 9 8 7 6 5 4 3 2 1

Library of Congress Control Number: 2015931421

ISBN 978-1-59373-155-7
e-book ISBN 978-1-59373-180-9

Designed by JDL
Printed in Canada

He was a big horse, proud and strong. His dark bay coat was the reddish-brown color of mahogany; his legs, mane, tail, and muzzle were coal black. But as he clip-clopped his way to the house at Eighth and Jackson Streets in the bustling prairie town of Springfield, Illinois, he did not know that he was trotting into history. His new owner was to become one of the most important of all American presidents. And Old Bob, the master's new horse, would be sharing in his story.

The new owner who greeted Old Bob was tall and gangly, with pant legs too short and coattails too long. The master's face had sharp gray eyes under eyebrows as fuzzy as

caterpillars. The master's hair was so deeply brown, it was almost black, and so coarse it was like Old Bob's own swishing tail. When the prairie breezes swept through, the manes of both horse and master blew haphazardly this way and that, and neither Old Bob nor Abraham Lincoln made any attempt at rearrangement.

Across the backyard ran three little boys, Bob, Willie, and Tad. They were eager to pet the new horse. They darted in and out between Old Bob's long strong legs just as they did when they romped with their long-legged father on the floor of their home. From the house waved the new master's wife, a woman with a plump round face and a calico apron over a fine dress she had stitched herself.

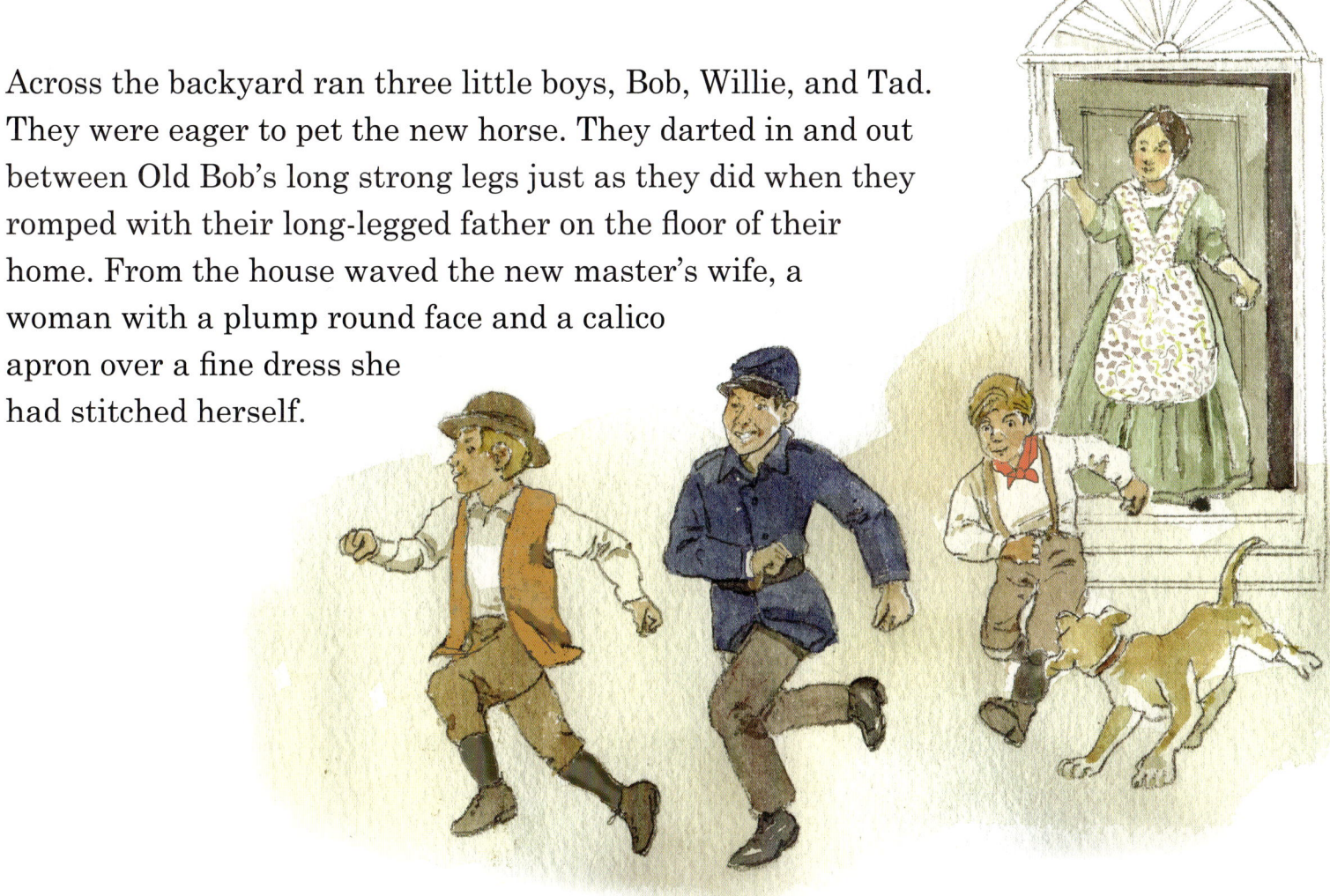

There was little time for Old Bob to get acquainted with the family, for spring had arrived, and Old Bob's new master had to be off right away. Abraham Lincoln was a lawyer, and for many years now, in spring and fall, he left home to practice law in the tiny villages of the Eighth Circuit that extended across eleven thousand square miles of central Illinois. By "riding the circuit," Lincoln could bring legal services to far-flung villagers without a local court. As he rode from one county seat to another, sometimes he traveled alone on horseback. Sometimes he hitched a buggy to his horse. More often he traveled in the company of other lawyers and judges.

Now horse and master journeyed across the wide prairie landscape that was familiar to both. In places the big bluestem and Indian grasses grew so high that even a tall man like Lincoln had to stand up in Old Bob's stirrups to see over them. Gophers, squirrels, and white-tailed deer parted the grasses below, and red-tailed hawks swooped across the blue skies above. In a few weeks farmers would be turning over the dark loamy earth for planting, and a few weeks after that, butterflies and bees would be fluttering around wildflowers like prairie coneflowers and black-eyed Susans. For now, horse and rider enjoyed the fragrance of lilacs perfuming the clean, fresh, windswept air of the prairie in spring.

Although the prairies were beautiful, Abe and Old Bob had their share of troubles while traveling. Streams lacked bridges, and the barely passable trails could hardly be called roads. After the spring thaw with its soaking rains, deep, thick, sucking mud threatened to bring down buggy wheels and even the sturdiest horse's legs. Sometimes Lincoln and Old Bob found themselves in the middle of nowhere during a thunderstorm without a shelter in sight. No wonder settlers were hailing the coming of the railroad, with its promise of swifter and more comfortable travel.

Old Bob and Lincoln became fast friends. Although Lincoln had traveled the circuit with other horses before, Old Bob was clearly special. There was something in his temperament that was like his master's: strong, calm, dependable. The way his ears pricked up to listen mirrored the intelligence of his master too. Old Bob soon recognized that his master loved animals by the way he stopped frequently at streams to water him or curried him carefully when they finally reached their night's lodging.

Abe and the other circuit riders on the prairie spent the night in tiny villages, sleeping on ropes or quilts, washing up in the mornings with a single pitcher and a solitary towel, and breakfasting on bitter coffee. In the larger towns, there was often a decrepit tavern for lodging where the travelers slept three or four together in flea-infested beds and with sometimes no more for dinner than cooked cabbage. In the evenings, the weary travelers occasionally revived themselves by attending local lectures or circuses, but more commonly they swapped tall tales before the tavern fire, spitting tobacco into boxes lined with sand. In fact, a chuckling companionship existed among the group of circuit riders. Although hardly an old man, when Lincoln rode the circuit on Old Bob he was in his mid- to late forties, and the younger lawyers jokingly called him "Old Abe," a nickname that Lincoln held for years and a name that matched his horse.

Lincoln liked to describe how his horse "Old Bob" got his name— to distinguish him from his son "Bob" at home. Abe slapped his knee as he told this story, joining in the hearty laughter with his own distinct laugh, a high-pitched whinny that weary Old Bob could identify from his crowded stable. They probably also laughed about his unique filing system, for out on the prairie Lincoln was known to use his tall stovepipe hat for stashing papers and documents.

Old Bob's alert ears probably stood straight up as Lincoln told the other circuit riders the story of the pig he had as a boy in Kentucky. This little pig was Lincoln's first pet. He carried it home in a sack fashioned from his own shirttail. He fed and pampered it. He taught the pig to play hide-and-seek and spoiled it with acorn treats. Perhaps Lincoln left out the part about the terrible day that his father butchered his pet for food, the day that sent the boy running off into the woods to avoid the dying squeals that ripped at his young heart.

Perhaps he told them the story of the dog he saved from drowning. Abe had grown into a young man by then, and he and his family made up a party of thirteen that was moving by wagon from Indiana to Illinois during a cold, damp March. Facing an ice-strewn river, the travelers realized that a submerged corduroy bridge offered only a treacherous path across. With great difficulty, Abe nudged the reluctant oxen onto the makeshift bridge. Halfway across, Abe suddenly heard the cries of the little dog stranded behind on the icy shore. Unable to bear the animal's helpless cries, Abe waded back across the icy currents to rescue the grateful animal.

Perhaps he told them the story of the turtle. Abe, largely self-taught, had experienced only brief periods of education as rough as the log cabins that passed for schools. During one of those occasional times, some of his school chums had been teasing a turtle, trying to force it out of its shell by placing hot coals on its back. Furious, Abe put the torture to a stop; later, he wrote an essay warning about "Cruelty to Animals."

Clearly Lincoln couldn't bear cruelty to animals. But he could not bear cruelty to human beings, either. On a flatboat trip down the Mississippi to deliver goods to New Orleans, the strapping young man had observed a group of slaves being sold at auction. It was the first time Lincoln had ever seen human beings treated like animals, and it made a powerful impression on him. He did not know it then, but one day in the future he would be able to right such a cruel and terrible wrong.

When Old Bob and Old Abe finally returned home after three months of absence, the two were greeted by the whoops and hurrahs of three sons and a wife who had dearly missed him. Even the neighbors hung over the fences, waving the travelers welcome as their cows mooed in the yard.

Carefully, Old Abe groomed his faithful horse, currying his haunches to loosen the dirt from their travels, picking the hooves clean of caked mud and debris while the boys tossed hay to one another in the stall and his neighbor declared to Lincoln, "You love your horse well."

Still, despite these happy returns, Old Abe and Old Bob were destined
for experiences other than circuit riding. And on May 18, 1860, a
hundred-gun salute heralded an announcement that electrified the
prairie city of Springfield: Mr. Abraham Lincoln, their
neighbor and friend, had been nominated by the
Republican party as candidate for president
of the United States. Surely Old Bob
whinnied with excitement as he saw
the bonfires

in the square and the lights in windows, as he heard the rocket flares and cheering crowds, and as he watched the Lincoln boys canvassing the neighborhoods shouting, "Vote for Old Abe."

Old Abe, in fact, had made a name for himself on the fiery national issue of slavery. The country had been experiencing unprecedented western expansion, and great controversies had arisen over whether those new territories should be organized as slave states or free states. The issue had grown so heated that southerners in the slaveholding states were threatening to leave the Union.

From the Hall of Representatives in the statehouse in Springfield in 1858, Lincoln made a famous speech that received national attention. It was called the "House Divided" speech, and in it he had declared that, like a divided house, the United States could not continue to exist if it were half slave and half free. This speech was followed by a series of famous debates with Senator Stephen A. Douglas in which Lincoln convincingly defended his anti-slavery position, garnering thousands of political followers in the process.

Although Lincoln was barely known in Washington, DC, and the rest of the country when he was nominated for the presidency in 1860, no one in Illinois was surprised, for as Old Abe and Old Bob had traveled around the state, they had developed many friendships. The people of Illinois had come to love Abe Lincoln as much as Lincoln loved his horse. Riding the circuit, Lincoln grew familiar with the citizens of Illinois, remembering by first name the farmers and their plots of lands as well as their parents, children, and pets. Through his many and varied jobs as postmaster, blacksmith, clerk, soldier, and surveyor, Abe had developed a reputation for fairness that would benefit him in the presidential election. Just like those of the hardworking people he encountered, his had been a hardscrabble life with few advantages and many losses.

When he won the presidential election in 1860, these common people embraced him as their own.

Everything changed quickly for Old Abe. Sadly, even the lives of the family's animals—including that of Old Bob—had to change. Old Bob was sent to an unfamiliar new stable in Springfield; Fido, the boys' dog, was sent to live with another family with boys.

On the cold, rainy morning of February 11, 1861, a heavyhearted Lincoln said good-bye to the people of Springfield from the platform of his departing train. Filled with emotion, he expressed his gratitude for their many kindnesses to him. Acknowledging the difficulties facing him as the leader of a country that was rapidly descending into civil war, he spoke of the dangerous future ahead. "I now leave," he said, "not knowing when, or whether ever, I may return, with a task before me greater than that which rested upon Washington . . ." To his dear neighbors, he concluded: "I bid you an affectionate farewell."

Almost immediately after he was inaugurated on March 4, 1861, the American Civil War began. Lincoln faced many difficulties across four years of war. He had to raise an army. He had to feed, clothe, and arm it. He had to suffer incompetent generals and defiant members of Congress. Worst of all, he had to deal with the North's many battlefield defeats in which thousands of young soldiers perished at battles called Bull Run, Antietam, Fredericksburg, and Cold Harbor.

During that terrible time, however, Old Abe's cares were often relieved by the presence of both children and animals. Knowing how much Lincoln loved cats, his new secretary of state presented him with a welcome-to-Washington gift of a pair of kittens. They climbed all over the president as he drafted documents or signed official papers. Later the White House family acquired a little dog named Jip, who often lunched with the president.

A White House tradition was launched when a weeping Tad burst into a White House meeting. Tad had formed a fast friendship that fall with a plump turkey he named "Jack." When he learned that Jack was to be killed for a holiday dinner, the boy was distraught. Lincoln likely thought back to the young boy whose father had slaughtered his own pet pig for food, so he wrote out an executive order sparing Jack's life. To this day, presidents often honor Jack by writing out a "pardon" for a turkey at Thanksgiving.

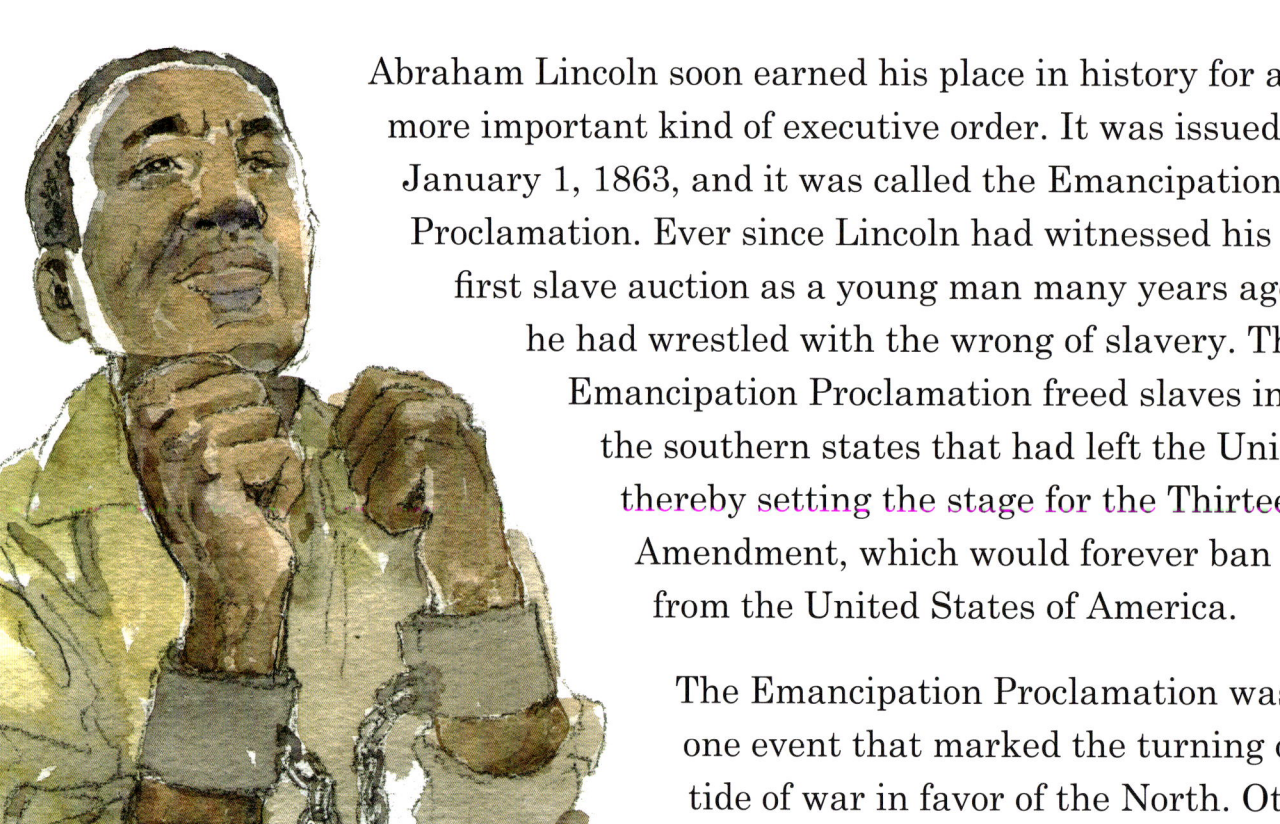

Abraham Lincoln soon earned his place in history for another, more important kind of executive order. It was issued on January 1, 1863, and it was called the Emancipation Proclamation. Ever since Lincoln had witnessed his first slave auction as a young man many years ago, he had wrestled with the wrong of slavery. The Emancipation Proclamation freed slaves in the southern states that had left the Union, thereby setting the stage for the Thirteenth Amendment, which would forever ban slavery from the United States of America.

The Emancipation Proclamation was only one event that marked the turning of the tide of war in favor of the North. Other events included the Battle of Gettysburg, the siege of Vicksburg, the burning of Atlanta, and the appointment of Ulysses S. Grant as general in chief of all US armies.

But the fact that the war was winding down did not decrease southern hatred of Lincoln. After all, he represented the defeat of their cause. Rumors of assassination swirled around the president, who often disregarded his own safety.

Once, when Lincoln was on a solitary night ride, a bullet whizzed so close to his head that it knocked off his hat. The startled horse and rider took off at a gallop, racing to safety.

Thankfully, however, on April 9, 1865, the war ended when General Ulysses S. Grant of the North and General Robert E. Lee of the South met to sign a formal end to hostilities at Appomattox Court House in Virginia. Finally the Civil War, which had cost more than six hundred thousand lives, was over.

Like communities all over the North, Springfield, Illinois, was jubilant. Lights glowed in windows, storefronts were draped with bunting, and naturally there had to be a parade. Suddenly everybody remembered Old Bob. He needed a place of honor in the parade.

Recognizing Old Bob's importance, someone, probably one of the ladies of Springfield, stitched a patriotic red, white, and blue blanket for Lincoln's favorite horse. Decorated with hundreds of tiny Union flags, the blanket was spread across Old Bob's sturdy back for the special event. As he flicked his tail on his march through Springfield, holding his pointed ears back and his head high, Old Abe's spirited horse likely whinnied with excitement, but remained calm as parade-goers who lined the route snatched the little flags from Old Bob's blanket to keep as souvenirs. Even the blanket itself was finally torn into tiny pieces as remembrances of this special day.

But all too quickly the nation's joy turned to despair. On April 14, 1865, an actor and disgruntled southerner named John Wilkes Booth assassinated President Lincoln while he was watching a play at Ford's Theatre in Washington, DC. The peace that Abraham Lincoln had worked so hard to achieve had been shattered.

The nation was plunged into mourning. Cities that had recently gone wild with celebration now went silent with shock. Torchlight festivals turned into torchlight vigils. Bells that had jangled in happiness tolled in sorrow. Storefronts were no longer festooned with red, white, and blue bunting but shadowed with the black crepe of bereavement.

And no city in newly peaceful America mourned more deeply than the residents of Springfield, Illinois. They had lost not only a president, but a resident, a neighbor, a friend.

For them, there was only one wave of consolation in the midst of this national tide of grief. It was the decision that Abraham Lincoln's body would be coming home. To Springfield.

As Lincoln's funeral train chugged along its route to Springfield, it stopped in Baltimore, Harrisburg, Philadelphia, New York, Albany, Buffalo, Cleveland, Columbus, Indianapolis, and Chicago. Throughout the seventeen-hundred-mile journey the railroad tracks were lined with weeping citizens. More than seven million Americans watched as the train passed by. Reaching Springfield at nine o'clock on the morning of May 3, 1865, Lincoln's body was taken to the Hall of the House of Representatives where more than seventy-five thousand citizens filed by to pay their final respects.

On the next day, Abraham Lincoln, Springfield's own, would be buried. He had left Springfield by train four years ago, wondering "when, or whether ever" he would return. He had once written that "in this sad world of ours, sorrow comes to all," often taking us "unawares." Lincoln's neighbors and friends had never expected a homecoming like this. This bitter sorrow had taken them unawares.

At dawn on Thursday, May 4, thirty-six guns fired, followed by a single shot every ten minutes until the procession to the cemetery got under way. Lincoln's body was carried in a hearse made of gold, silver, and crystal and bearing a silver plate engraved with his initials and surrounded by a silver wreath with thirty-six stars. The hearse was drawn by six gleaming black horses with silver harnesses. Bouquets of spring flowers plucked from the gardens of Springfield neighbors and friends were strewn across the coffin.

But behind the hearse, occupying a sacred place of honor, marched a proud bay horse with a sloping back and coal-black points. Old Bob had been curried and washed and brushed that morning until his coat gleamed.

Atop his head was a magnificent headdress; across his strong haunches had been draped a black blanket fringed with tassels.

On this important occasion, Old Bob had been chosen to serve an important function. He would fill the role of the riderless horse—one of the highest honors given to the fallen. The riderless horse symbolized that the valiant commander would ride no more. As commander in chief during the Civil War, Old Bob's master had served his country well. Now Old Bob would well serve his master for one final time. To the sad, steady beat of muffled drums, the cortege began to move through Old Abe and Old Bob's beloved Springfield. Old Bob was escorting his master on his final ride home.

Fittingly, Old Bob was led by the Reverend Henry Brown, an African American minister who had often done odd jobs for the Lincolns. Marching directly behind the coffin and linked together were two subjects of Lincoln's famous compassion, one human, the other animal. Behind Old Bob and Reverend Brown walked some of Lincoln's relatives and friends, and after that walked congresspersons, ministers, governors, and ordinary citizens, among whom were many blacks who had been freed by Lincoln's Emancipation Proclamation.

It was unseasonably warm that day, the heat intensifying the scent of lilacs in the spring prairie air. Old Bob proudly marched behind the hearse as it rumbled east on Washington Street and south on Eighth Street past the Lincoln home. All over Springfield, mourning drapery hung from rooftops like widows' veils over the eyes of windows. Citizens crowded the funeral route and even sat on rooftops. Souvenir hunters snatched blossoms from the apple tree of Lincoln's Springfield home, and they grabbed at the mane and tail of Old Bob, hoping to add a famous horsehair to their scrapbook collections. Then the cortege marched past the governor's mansion, finally undertaking the long final walk to the eastern end of Oak Ridge Cemetery far from town.

The cemetery was a lovely, quiet spot in which two tree-lined ridges were parted by a babbling brook. Under the evergreen arch at the entrance to the cemetery, Old Bob halted. Around him like a vast sea of grass stretched the prairie landscape with its gophers and its deer, its squirrels and red-tailed hawks. Even now, farmers were turning over the dark loamy earth for planting, and in a few weeks butterflies and bees would be fluttering around wildflowers such as prairie coneflowers and black-eyed Susans. Sadly, the wild strawberries soon to be in season would no longer stain the lips of Old Bob's master.

Even so, as the prayers and the music began, as the fragrance of lilacs perfumed the air, as the citizens of Springfield listened to the words of the Second Inaugural Address in which their friend had imagined a reunited union with "malice toward none" and "charity for all," the remembered life of Old Bob's master was taking shape.

Already that life was standing as tall in the American imagination
as the prairie grasses from which it had sprung. Old Bob,
whose hooves had carried his master across that
prairie landscape countless times,
had now escorted his master
on his final ride. Standing
at attention among the
mourners, observing a
respectful silence in honor
of the man who had
shown such compassion
to all of creation, both
animal and human,
Old Bob likely offered a
final neigh or a whinny,
blessing his master with
an affectionate farewell.